The Call of Creation

NATURE'S INVITATION TO WORSHIP

JOHN MACMURRAY

CREATION CALENDARS, INC. EAGLE CREEK, OREGON

The debt that I owe to so many for their help and encouragement along my path grows daily. To Bob and Eric who have joined me most often—you lighten my load, literally and figuratively. To the good people of Good Shepherd Community Church—you humble me with your prayers and support. To my family—you have contributed to my life in so many ways. Take pleasure in what God has done through you, in me. To my children, Chris, Elle, and Cassy—thank you for making the trip home the most exciting part of my journey. Remember, the sunset is God's final brush strokes on the canvas He calls today. To my wife Terri—your unwavering love and loyalty means more than I can express. Thank you from the bottom of my socks! And finally to my God, the Creator of this wonderful beauty we call nature. May You be praised through this offering.

John MacMurray
c/o Creation Calendars, Inc.
32370 S.E. Judd Road
Eagle Creek, Oregon 97022

THE CALL OF CREATION
published by Creation Calendars, Inc.

© 2005 by John MacMurray
International Standard Book Number: 0-9768405-1-0

Design by Wisner Design, Inc.

Scripture quotations are from:
The Holy Bible, New International Version
© 1973, 1978, 1984 by the International Bible Society
used by permission of Zondervan Bible Publishers

Printed in China

ALL RIGHTS RESERVED
No part of this publication may be reproduced, stored in a retrieval system, or transmitted, in any form or by any means—electronic, mechanical, photocopying, recording, or otherwise—without prior written permission.

For information:
CREATION CALENDARS, INC.
32370 S.E. JUDD ROAD
EAGLE CREEK, OREGON 97022

www.creationcalendars.com

For my children; Chris, Elle, and Cassy.

May you see our Father's Glory

more clearly through the lens of nature's beauty.

You who have made your dwelling fair

With flowers below, above with starry lights

And set your altars everywhere—

On mountain heights,

In woodlands dim with many a dream

In valleys bright with springs,

An on the curving capes of every stream:

You who have taken to yourself the wings

Of morning, to abide

Upon the secret places of the sea,

An on far islands, where the tide

Visits the beauty of untrodden shores,

Waiting for worshippers to come to be

In thy great out-of-doors!

To you I turn, to you I make my prayer,

God of the open air.

HENRY VAN DYKE

INTRODUCTION

I woke to an incessant, annoying sound, like a microscopic Cessna flying around my head. Perhaps a choir of mosquitoes singing bug versions of Irish drinking songs. Maybe drunk mosquitoes flying a Cessna. But this sound was *louder*.

I attempted to ignore the intrusion. Time, in the dreamscape of my semi-conscious, had become distorted. For what seemed like an hour my mind struggled with visions of bugs and planes. Slowly, a thought edged its way into my mind; bugs do not fly planes…do they?

I sat up, still groggy, and in a reflex motion swatted the alarm clock; vague notions of mosquitoes not yet dispersed. *"Where am I?" "Why is it still dark?"* My mind was clearing slowly. I was in the bow of a boat anchored in a cove of Prince William Sound, Alaska. It was 3:00 AM. I groaned, wishing to remain within the warm embrace of my sleeping bag. I confess I do not particularly like this part of my job. I love the outdoors. And taking pictures is great. But getting out of bed in the middle of what I regard to be essential sleep time with peanut butter for a brain and blocks of ice for feet is something best left for nocturnal creatures.

My plan was to capture the dawn light in the pristine Alaskan wilderness. My dazed mind was struggling to win its debate with my body. So much for the glamour of being a landscape photographer I thought. But if I didn't get out of bed I might, as my friends so often remind me, have to get a real job. I shuddered, and remembered how fortunate I really am.

Despite my best attempts at being a complete clod, I stumbled out of the bow to prepare for my photographic excursion. As I began stuffing my pockets with fruit and cookies, I glanced outside and my heart sank.

When I had gone to bed the sky was clear. Now, clouds, so typical of Alaska, had invaded the area. What had been the motivation that finally dragged me out of bed had vanished. In the faint light it was difficult to evaluate the conditions. Clouds are both blessings and curses. They can reflect light with beautiful, even dramatic results, or they can block it like blobs of boring gray.

Sometimes nature photography is like a percentage game. Will the fog eventually clear, or is a storm front moving in? I reminded myself of those times when light breaks through and puts purple on glaciers and fire in clouds. I wondered which it would be as I loaded my equipment into the raft tied to the stern of the boat.

Descending into the zodiac, the water in the Sound was unusually still. The air was quiet, chilly, and damp. The combination seemed to add reverence to the moment. Almost like nature was telling me to hush and be still with her. But preoccupied with my task, I ignored the gentle invitation.

Small patches of clearing allowed the first light of dawn to illuminate the watery scene. Gray clouds were reflected in the stillness of the water, bathing the whole landscape in a monochromatic light. A familiar sense of peace and tranquility, that always seems to accompany me on early morning trips into wilderness, lifted my spirits. Hope was rekindled within me for the possibility of a good photograph. Even the sound of the little three horse-power engine disturbing the stillness wasn't enough to dampen the anticipation growing in my heart.

I proceeded to navigate the raft along the shoreline, about forty yards from its bank. Dense, virgin evergreens crowded the shoreline in all directions. Their pungent aroma aroused me with the purity of the place. A forest in all of its magnificence was stretched before me. More than just anticipation, a growing sense of reverence to the beauty surrounding me stirred my soul. In the distance, majestic peaks were shrouded in robes of silver. And though the clouds were steadily descending, shafts of light were beginning to pierce the silver lining and streak across the landscape, creating isolated jewels shimmering on the surface of the water. Other than the boat I had slept on and the raft I was in, there wasn't a trace of human intrusion anywhere. I was alone in this incredible place watching Nature awaken and reveal the beauty that had been veiled in night's darkness.

My excitement was winning the battle against the demons of lethargy which had tried to trap me in my bed. But the reality of my job abruptly interrupted my musings. I realized I needed to find a suitable place to land the raft in order to make an attempt to capture on film the drama unfolding around me. My light was coming quickly, and I felt the urgency of my task.

Dawn photographs are taken through small windows of time shortly before and after the sun breaks the horizon. The majority of great landscape photographs are taken at first and last light. I have photographed hundreds of sunrises. And though the quality of the light and color has varied greatly (as do my photographs), the morning is still beautiful to me. The magnitude of the landscape is not something a person becomes completely calloused to. And yet, there are times when watching the day begin feels something more like pleasurable business than pleasurable pleasure. But not on this day. The glory that was appearing before me was amazing. My work was taking a back seat to pleasure. Whatever my expectations had been for the images I might encounter that morning, they were about to change significantly.

Out of the corner of my eye, I noticed movement at the top of a tree. A giant bald eagle spread its powerful wings and lunged into space. Without one thrust from his impressive wings, he descended effortlessly toward the water. His flight took him away from the shore, perpendicular to it, only thirty feet or so in front of my raft. His wing span was close to 7 feet across and his talons were considerably larger than my hands. He was gliding inches above the surface of the water. As the eagle came into my direct line, he swiveled his regal head and his brilliant eyes stared straight into mine. His piercing look was not that of a hunter, fishing for breakfast. It was, I suppose, more curiosity than anything else. He was investigating this strange object along the water producing such an annoying noise.

He continued gracefully along the water's surface for another thirty yards and ascended in an elegant arc back toward my raft. By this time, I had shut down the motor to an idle. Captivated, I jerked around in the zodiac, straining my neck upward in fascination as with two mighty thrusts, he returned to his perch atop the evergreen.

As a photographer, frustration tainted what I had experienced. No image. No record of the event. I am acutely aware of the thousands of photographers who would have relinquished a great deal of their personal worth to be present, camera ready, at what I had experienced.

I work with what is called a large format camera, which requires a tripod and a considerable amount of time to assemble. Even if I had the presence of mind to attempt to set up my camera, the soft bottom of the zodiac would have precluded erecting my tripod. But this particular morning was calling me to something far greater than a mere picture.

As a person, not just a photographer, who is growing to appreciate our world, I was awed. Unmoving, I sat and watched the eagle, still pondering the incredible encounter. The encounter seemed semi-casual, almost friendly. A sort of "welcome to my domain" flight. But more than friendly, it was personal. Intensely personal. It was the eagle and me in the midst of a spectacular and majestic setting. Nothing else stirred. Not even the wind.

As I resumed my course along the banks of Prince William Sound, I realized I was feeling not just happy (that would be far too trite), but more like deeply content—even fulfilled. Yet I had not taken a single photograph, which was, in fact, my purpose for waking at such a horrible hour. The word I searched for to describe my feelings was, I believe, inspired. Truly. The encounter had motivated me beyond a task or goal. It had called me to reverence. But, to revere the eagle was absurd. Respect the eagle—most certainly. What I was feeling was greater than respect. Nature had called me that morning to worship.

There seems to be something wonderfully unique about the nature of human beings. We alone, from among all the creatures on this planet, view nature with an appreciation for its beauty. We are interested in nature not only in a functional sense, as all other creatures are, but in an aesthetic sense as well. And this, as far as I can tell, is universal among the human species. The feelings I experienced that morning would have been essentially the same for anyone else who might have been in my place. We long for and crave the beauty that surrounds us. We use words such as majestic, grandeur, splendor, and awesome to describe the beauty of nature. So this begs the question, *why is nature so beautiful to us?*

As I travel throughout our world, continuing to enjoy and appreciate what I photograph, I have become thoroughly convinced that our natural world is a creation of supernatural origin. And that I, along with everyone else, have been created in such a way as to perceive beauty in our natural world and respond in appreciation for it. Consequently, I have come to believe the reverence and awe that I experience in the natural world is not simply for the things I see. It is for the God who made them. It is the Creator God that nature, in all of its splendor and magnificence, compellingly points us toward. In my fertile imagination I suspect that if all the flora and fauna of our world could speak as we do they would with a singular, collective voice shout to us, "Don't worship us! Worship our Designer and Maker!" This is, I believe, why nature universally stirs in us a common appreciation for its beauty. It is inviting us everyday, every time we see it or experience it, to worship the One who made it.

With this collection of photographs, I have attempted to capture this "visual voice" of Nature's beauty. As with all attempts at representing reality with ink and paper, this one falls short of its mark. Nonetheless, my hope is that as you peruse the images within these pages you too will hear Nature's call and respond to its invitation. "Come and worship our God and Maker."

JOHN MACMURRAY

MAJESTY

There are times in my wanderings when light, form, and color combine in such a harmony that it takes my breath away. At other times, the sheer immensity or grandeur of a place gives me more than a pause, I feel wonder and awe. It is at these moments that I am confronted with the majesty of Nature. It may be mountain peaks bathed in sunlight and robed with clouds. Or sunbeams bursting from behind a cloud and washing over the landscape with a yellow, crimson glow. However nature reveals it's majesty we take pleasure in it.

And though our responses may vary, we all sense, to some degree, a common perspective. We feel small.

I believe the Creator of this magnificent beauty has "wired" us this way. He welcomes the comparison of these awe-inspiring moments to Himself. So that when I am stimulated by what I see that I consider great, I would then compare it to the One who made it and know in the depth of my being that He is immeasurably greater. If this is true, then the beauty and majesty we find in nature is the continuing, open invitation to stand in awe and worship.

For me, the world of nature bears spectacular witness to the imaginative genius of our Creator.

PHILIP YANCEY

MT. BAKER, WASHINGTON

Grey Glacier, Chile

Cramer Lake, Sawtooth Wilderness, Idaho

The heavens declare the glory of God; the skies proclaim the work of his hands.
Day after day they pour forth speech; night after night they display knowledge.
There is no speech or language where their voice is not heard.

PSALM 19:1–3

Sierra Nevada Range, California

Cirque of the Towers, Wind River Range, Wyoming

Ecola State Park, Oregon

Cloudy Pass, Glacier Peak Wilderness, Washington

MT. HOOD, OREGON

JOSHUA TREE, NEVADA

I thank Thee, my Creator and Lord,
that Thou hast given me this joy in Thy creation,
this delight in the works of Thy hands.

JOHANN KEPLER

Bryce Canyon National Park, Utah

Moraine Lake, Banff National Park, Canada

Olympic National Park, Washington

Mt. Saint Helens, Washington

Before the mountains were born
or you brought forth the earth and the world,
from everlasting to everlasting you are God.

PSALM 90:2

MT. JEFFERSON, OREGON

Grand Canyon National Park, Arizona

Grand Teton National Park, Wyoming

Nevada Falls, Yosemite National Park, California

Why does so much of it look almost as if

it were designed...to please the eye,

and for no other reason?

GORDON STAINFORTH

MT. WILSON, COLORADO

GRAND CANYON NATIONAL PARK, ARIZONA

Willamette National Forest, Oregon

Berg Lake, Mt. Robson Provincial Park, Canada

This glorious valley might well be called a church,
for every lover of the great Creator who comes
within the broad overwhelming influences of the place
fails not to worship as they never did before.

JOHN MUIR

Yoho National Park, Canada

El Captain, Yosemite National Park, California

Logan Meadow, Glacier National Park, Montana

HECETA HEAD, OREGON

To the extent we deny God, we reduce ourselves to accidental beings
on a temporary planet in a random universe expanding into nowhere.
To the extent we have a sense of the existence of God,
we discover creation confessing God's being
and see the beauty as a confession of God.

JIM FORREST

Wonder Lake, Denali National Park, Alaska

Glacier Peak Wilderness, Washington

Lake O'Hara, Yoho National Park, Canada

Bays Lake and Mt. Jefferson, Oregon

Yosemite National Park, California

Smith Rocks State Park, Oregon

Who has measured the waters in the hollow of his hand,

or with the breadth of his hand marked off the heavens?

Who has held the dust of the earth in a basket, or weighed the mountains

on the scales and the hills in a balance?... Do you not know? Have you not heard?

The Lord is the everlasting God, the Creator of the ends of the earth.

ISAIAH 40:12, 28

Maroon Bells, Colorado

Torres Del Paine National Park, Chile

Key Summit, Fiordland National Park, New Zealand

Eiger Peak, Switzerland

It is awesome and wonderful

to behold the character of the Creator

in what He has made...

HUGH NORMAN ROSS

BERCHTESGADEN NATIONAL PARK, GERMANY

MT. RAINIER NATIONAL PARK, WASHINGTON

Monument Valley, Arizona

SERENITY

I remember my first hike to a small waterfall in Oregon. As I approached the waterfall the trail opened up into a little alcove of fir trees and lush green. Water was pouring from a cut in the rock about 80 feet above the path and descending into a crystal stream that cut its way through maples and ferns along its banks. Nothing but the water was heard. A gentle breeze from the mist caused the leaves to sway. Though I was 20 minutes from the highway, I had entered another world. A secret place where time had been suspended. The trees surrounded me like guardians, as I sat down, a willing captive to this special place. Wind and water soothed my soul and I experienced a peace that transcended anything I could manufacture. Gratitude stirred deep within me. There was pleasure in the moment that I didn't want to end. The tranquillity of the landscape beckoned me to more than simply rest or relaxation.

Why do we long for places like these? Certainly we all seek a measure of relief from our everyday stress. But it is more than that. We feel a harmony and a sense of belonging with our world when nature confronts us this way. We experience what I would call presence—the presence of the Creator. Nature is just the herald inviting us to meet with Him in His garden. The poet said it well, "The Lord is my shepherd, I shall not want. He makes me lie down in green pastures; He leads me beside quiet waters. He restores my soul."

I knew I would return to this waterfall regardless of any photo possibilities. And in fact, I have.

Be still,

and know

that I am God.

PSALM 46:10

Punchbowl Falls, Oregon

Sedona, Arizona

Ansel Adams Wilderness, California

Look at the beauty of nature around us...
you can only be filled with wonder at the wisdom of a Creator,
who, first of all, had the sense of beauty to do it,
and then the technical ability.

ARTHUR E. WILDER-SMITH

Fallen Leaves, Maine

Lake Gunn, Fiordland National Park, New Zealand

Redwood National Park, California

Pyramid Lake, Nevada

The outdoors has been to me more and more a great cathedral
in which God could be spoken to and heard from...

GEORGE WASHINGTON CARVER

COLUMBIA RIVER, OREGON

GLEN ETIVE, SCOTLAND

Chester County, Pennsylvania

WAIKOLOA, HAWAII

Lake Wanaka, New Zealand

Double Arch, Arches National Park, Utah

Shenandoah National Park, Virginia

Oneonta Gorge, Oregon

Great are the works of the Lord;

they are pondered by all who delight in them.

PSALM 111:2

MT. TRIGLAV, SLOVENIA

TODD LAKE AND MT. BACHELOR, OREGON

Come, let us bow down in worship,

let us kneel before the Lord our Maker.

PSALM 95:6

Upper Multnomah Falls, Oregon

Three Sisters Wilderness, Oregon

Cape Meares, Oregon

Wallowa Lake, Oregon

Noosa National Park, Australia

Olympic National Park, Washington

Thy wisdom, Thy power, and Thy goodness
are everywhere clearly seen; in the air and in the water,
in the heavens and on the earth....Praised be Thy Name forever.

BENJAMIN FRANKLIN

Long Pond, Maine

Clackamas River, Oregon

O Lord; I sing for joy at the works of your hands.

PSALM 92:4

OLYMPIC NATIONAL PARK, WASHINGTON

ACADIA NATIONAL PARK, MAINE

GRINDELWALD, SWITZERLAND

TORONGO RIVER, AUSTRALIA

Columbia River Gorge, Oregon

Lake Tahoe, Nevada

APPENDIX

Front Jacket Cover and Page 45   Torres del Paine, Chile

I had been hiking in the mountains of Patagonia for several days in what was for the most part, terrible weather. When it finally cleared I hiked out of the mountains in an attempt to photograph the best view in the park. I was scouting for a location for the next morning when I met a German couple interested in photography. We spent the remainder of the day exploring the park while I shared with them photographic tips. After dinner they suggested I rent a room where they were staying, about 9 miles away. The thought of a hot shower and a bed was hard to resist. Later, when we said good night they told me they were not going to the lake.

So, five hours later I awoke, packed my gear, and began hiking. After two hours it became obvious I wouldn't make it to the lake in time for the sunrise. In the faint pre-dawn light I could see the eastern horizon was clear and wispy clouds had stalled, clinging to the peaks. It was developing into an incredible sunrise. Dejection and frustration swept over me like a flood. About 15 minutes before the sun came up headlights approached from behind me. I stood in the middle of the road and waved for the truck to stop. I'm not sure what convinced him, the panic on my face or the pathetic begging of my voice, but he showed kindness and agreed to drive me the final 3 miles. I ran to the lake edge and took this photo. After a few more pictures I rested in the stillness, mesmerized by the drama unfolding before me. The sun was raising the curtain on one of the most awesome scenes I had ever witnessed. So incredible it appeared surreal. In those quiet moments, realizing how close I came to missing this spectacle, gratitude filled my heart and tears filled my eyes. I was a blessed man. It occurred to me that God had brought me 9000 miles for *this* moment. And I began to worship Him. Incidentally, the next car on the road was 3½ hours later!

Title Page   Black Mountain Gap, NC

This photograph reminds me that I don't always get the image I expect. But if I'm patient, many times I will get an image that is just as good or better. It was late October and I was in North Carolina for the last autumn color. At days end, I drove up to the Gap hoping for a good sunset. My attention was focused primarily to the West waiting for color that never materialized. I glanced to the North and saw bare trees silhouetted against sunlit clouds and immediately knew *that* was my picture for the night. I love being surprised by nature!

Dedication Page   Springvale, ME

I discovered this creek as I was searching for autumn foliage in Maine. It took quite a bit of time to set my camera for this picture. The depth of field required for the leaves and water to both be in focus was between f45 and f64. I wanted a long exposure to make the water appear as though it was moving in the image. But with such a long exposure I had to wait a long time for the light and wind to cooperate so that I could expose the film correctly and still have a sharp image. I was really pleased with the way it turned out. The photo almost looks three dimensional.

Page 11   Grinnell Lake, Glacier National Park, MT

Eric, Bob and I had gone hiking in Waterton National Park, which is the Canadian side of Glacier National Park. We had already paid for that night's camp site in Glacier so that we could be at Grinnell for the sunrise. On our return from Waterton we arrived at the border to find the gate locked and the border closed. Between sleeping in the car and on the pavement, it made for a miserable night waiting for the US agents to open the gate. Once back in our home country we drove like maniacs and practically ran up the trail to take this photo while the light was still good.

Page 13   Mt. Baker, WA

One of my favorite areas of the Cascade Range is along the border of Canada. Mt. Baker is the highest mountain in that region and is covered with glacial ice all year. I have hiked to Skyline Divide twice before, but on both occasions my timing was off and I missed the flowers in bloom. On this cloudless, brilliant day I was rewarded with a spectacular display of wildflowers along the Ridge. I guess the third time was the charm.

Page 14   Grey Glacier, Chile

After hiking about 9 miles in miserable weather, (rain, wind, thunder, lightning, snow, hail) we finally arrived at the camp site near the terminus of the Grey Glacier, which reaches out from the Patagonia Ice Cap. The next day was mainly overcast but the skies were clearing. I wanted to get an image that captured the drama of the glacier. Yet, as the sun began to peek out, I became fascinated by the deep blue in the ice. To get both the drama and the amazing blue I took this shot from a ridge above the glacier, looking down on it. Due to the difficulty of the exposure I was unsure whether my image would turn out. So, when I returned to the States and developed the image, I was thrilled.

Page 15   Cramer Lake, Sawtooth Wilderness, ID

Learning the angles of sunlight on a particular landscape as it moves along its path through the course of the day is part of my exploration and investigative work. Discovering this helped me determine how I would photograph the waterfall. I waited for the last of evening's light on the fall itself before I made this image. Then I jumped off the rock for my evening bath. One of the coldest lakes I ever swam in!

Page 16   Sunset over the Sierras, CA

I was in Reno, NV when I noticed the sky was clearing. I was particularly interested in the form and direction of the clouds. I hopped into my rental car and began chasing the clearing on the horizon. After 2 hours of driving like a wildman, and with the show about to begin, I found a huge Ponderosa pine tree facing the Sierra Range. I've seen maybe 6 sunsets like this; when the color in the clouds stretches 180 degrees, from horizon to horizon. I love the nuance of the different colors. It was spectacular!

PAGE 17   CIRQUE OF THE TOWERS, WIND RIVER RANGE, WY

In my opinion, The Cirque is in the top ten of "coolest places to backpack". It is a climbers' paradise. Yet, I have never seen a photograph that does it justice (including mine). It is one of those rare locations that is too big for the camera to take in. That said, I'm very pleased with this image. The sheer rock faces that dramatically point to the sky are breathtaking to me. And I love the starkness of the granite contrasted with the flowers.

PAGE 18   ECOLA STATE PARK, OR

If you ever visit Oregon and desire to see the ocean, this is where you must come. No self respecting tour guide or friend would let you miss this glorious view. No matter the time of day, the season of the year, or the condition of the weather, this vista is stunning. On a coastline that stretches for nearly 350 miles, it is arguably, (though there is no argument in my house) the most spectacular view of the Oregon coast you will find. I have lingered here for hours drinking the glory of this vista in. I hope this image conveys some of that majesty to you.

PAGE 19   CLOUDY PASS, GLACIER PEAK WILDERNESS, WA

Our last evening in Glacier Peak Wilderness Bob and I camped at Cloudy Pass. The next morning we needed to hike about 10 miles to catch a bus that took us to a boat that ferried us out Lake Chelan to our car. I thought I had brought enough film for our 5 day trip. But I only had three sheets of film left. Naturally, the next morning brought most amazing clouds of our visit! The cloud formations seemed to follow us. Always at the right angles, the clouds lingered around the most dramatic peaks far longer than usual. I feel fortunate to have this image but disappointed that so many are only a memory. This ranks in my top ten photographic blunders, but produced a cardinal rule. Always have enough film!

PAGE 20   MT. HOOD, OR

I have made more images of Mt. Hood than any other mountain. This is due in large part to my proximity to it. I see the mountain every day out my bedroom window. I should say every clear day. Notwithstanding, Mt. Hood is a beautiful peak. The fact that I never grow tired of looking at it is proof to its beauty. There are two reasons why I feel this way. First, no matter what side you view the mountain from, whether it's north or south, east or west, or anywhere in between, it retains an incredible symmetry. Yet, when you view the mountain from these different vantage points rarely does it look like the same mountain. This image I made from the roof of my car off Highway 35.

PAGE 21   JOSHUA TREE, NV

I was exploring photographic possibilities around Mt. Charleston outside of Las Vegas, NV. The drama of the clouds initially drew me to this scene. I found one of the trees that still had a bloom and waited until the last possible moment as the shadows advanced toward the tree. If you look closely, you'll see the foreground on the right side of the image is already in shadow. Thirty seconds after I took the picture the sunlight was gone.

PAGE 22   BRYCE CANYON NATIONAL PARK, UT

I have told many people that if I didn't live in the Northwest, my first choice in the U.S. would be southern Utah. The topography, colors, and forms are some of the most unique in the world. Bryce Canyon is an example, though only a fraction, of the incredible beauty that lies in the southern half of this state. I had been working in Zion the previous two days where the temperature was a delightful 75 degrees. This morning at Bryce was a balmy 17 degrees! I used a pair of socks as gloves to keep my hands warm. Though I got an "F" for preparedness, I took an "A" for improvisation.

PAGE 23   MORAINE LAKE, BANFF NATIONAL PARK, CANADA

The Valley of the Ten Peaks is one of my favorite places. Bob and I intended to hike into Larch Valley to photograph autumn's display of golden needles. As we approached the lake from the parking lot I noticed the cirrus clouds drifting overhead. I detoured over to the lake outlet and saw the clouds were positioned perfectly over the peaks. I scrambled up the rocks and made this image. Unbelievable blue! I love this place!

PAGE 24   LUPINE, OLYMPIC NATIONAL PARK, WA

I had spent the night camped at Deer Park. When I saw the awesome clouds the next morning I began looking for something to photograph where I could include them. I came around a bend and almost missed this meadow of lupine. When the dust cleared from my sudden stop I realized this was my photo. The clouds dictated which direction I would shoot. The mountains and meadow lined up perfectly!

PAGE 25   MT ST HELENS, WA

This was taken on a particularly brilliant September day in the Northwest. One of my best friends, Randy Thompson, was visiting from the east coast. So, I played tourist guide and took him to see Mt. St. Helens. We had a great time of fellowship during our three hour drive. The carnage left by the eruption in 1980 is unbelievable. I made a remark to that effect and I remember Randy's reply. He said, "Imagine the power it took to make and hold this mountain together!" We were both reminded of the awesomeness of our Creator. The Scripture says "All things were created by Him and in Him all things hold together." Amazing!

PAGE 26   MT. JEFFERSON, OR

After several days of rain in a row, which is typical of Oregon in the winter, the weather report predicted clearing skies. I knew that the copious amounts of rain were simultaneously several feet of snow in the mountains. This picture is actually taken from near Timberline Lodge on Mt. Hood looking due south at the Cascade Range. The sky and clouds cooperated to provide a gorgeous scene on this rare winter morning. By the way, it was 12 degrees when I took this picture.

PAGE 27 GRAND CANYON, AZ

I have been to the Grand Canyon at least 15 times in the last 20 years. It never grows old to me. In fact it holds a special place in my heart with regard to my journey both spiritually and photographically. (See my first book, *By Chance? Landscapes from the Canvas of the Creator*) But this particular trip was the first time my family had ever seen this incredible natural wonder. I took them late in the afternoon so that they could see the changing colors on the walls as the sun lowered in the sky. I took this picture with my family at my side. We stayed until the sun's final rays left the canyon. Then we ate some ice cream and poked around the gift shop. It is for me a memorial of sorts. It serves as a reminder that I am a blessed man!

PAGE 28 GRAND TETON NATIONAL PARK, WY

My good friend Eric Showell has joined me on several photo adventures. This trip remains one of our favorites. We had spent three nights backpacking in the Park. This particular afternoon we were leaving Lake Solitude to camp in a different area. I don't usually photograph in the middle of the day because of the harsh sunlight. But, as we continued down the trail these awesome looking clouds drifted behind the Grand Teton, which loomed in front of us. It was too good to pass by, so I unpacked my camera and took this image.

PAGE 29 NEVADA FALLS, YOSEMITE NATIONAL PARK, CA

This is a moderate hike from the valley floor that rewards you with a fantastic view. It was a beautiful spring day and the Merced River was pouring over the falls. At the top of the falls I remember eating a snack while lying in the sun. I gazed at Liberty Dome and the back of Half Dome and listened to the rapids about forty feet away. About 15 people joined in my marvelous fortune of being in Yosemite that day. I waited for the right light, walked the trail to the south, and took this shot. Tough to go wrong here!

PAGE 30 MT. WILSON, CO

My first autumn as a professional photographer I journeyed to Colorado for the color of the aspens. The weather was perfect. I found this spot while exploring the Telluride area of the Rockies. This trip was foundational in my realization of how fortunate I am. It reinforced for me the great joy and pleasure I receive from my work.

PAGE 31 GRAND CANYON NATIONAL PARK, AZ

I was in Arizona in mid March to photograph the desert in bloom. My third night there the weather report called for eighteen inches of snow at the Grand Canyon with clearing skies over the next 24 hours. This was music to my ears so I immediately left the Phoenix area and drove to the Canyon. When I arrived late that afternoon a foot of snow had accumulated and it was still snowing. I slept in my car and the next morning woke to a clear blue sky and $1\frac{1}{2}$ feet of fresh snow. God bless the weatherman (there have been times I've wanted God to curse the weatherman)!

PAGE 32 WILLAMETTE NATIONAL FOREST, OR

This is one of those photos that I wasn't looking for. I was driving down a back road in the Cascade Range east of Salem when I happened to pass this waterfall. I almost missed it. I love the green and the texture of the moss. I could sit at this spot on a regular basis.

PAGE 33 BERG LAKE, MT. ROBSON PROVINCIAL PARK, CANADA

Having received a call from Bob and Sandra Dorsey who were vacationing in Canada, my friend Eric and I made the 12 hour drive from Portland and arrived the next morning at the trail head to Berg Lake, which sits at the foot of Mt. Robson, the tallest mountain in the Canadian Rockies. With only 30 minutes sleep we began the 20 km hike. It was a sunny, hot day and the infamous black flies of that region had assembled in force to assault anyone attempting the trail. Whenever we stopped for a break, biting flies would attack our exposed skin with ferocity. Combined with our lack of sleep, the flies turned our hike into a grueling and tortuous effort. When we finally arrived at the lake the flies disappeared and we enjoyed a relaxing dinner with a stunning view! I worked until the sun left the mountain. Exhausted, I returned to our tent anticipating the photo possibilities the next morning. At 5:00 am, eight hours (which seemed like eight minutes) later, I woke up exactly as I had fallen asleep. I hadn't moved. The next two hours I enjoyed a serenity and grandeur that made all the effort worthwhile. When I finished working we packed up camp and began the long return to our vehicles. The last half of our trek was in a thunderstorm, which soaked just about everything in our packs.

PAGE 34 LAKE MCARTHUR, YOHO NATIONAL PARK, CANADA

This picture was taken from the Odaray highline trail in the Lake O'Hara region of the Canadian Rockies. It was a beautiful September day and the larch trees' needles had turned brilliant yellow. From this perspective they look like a yellow carpet on the valley floor. Again, I played the game of patience. Waiting until the last possible moment to take the photo before the shadow covered the color of the trees. This area makes it into my top ten places I've been backpacking. I think this vista shows why!

PAGE 35 EL CAPTAIN, YOSEMITE NATIONAL PARK, CA

It is difficult to capture the presence El Captain has in Yosemite Valley. This view across the Merced river in early morning is one of my favorites. It is both humbling and enthralling to look at its massive form from directly beneath. This perspective gives the mountain a throne-like appearance. I wonder if this was where John Muir stood when he referred to the Valley as a "cathedral"? I love the fog still burning off the eastern flank.

PAGE 36 LOGAN MEADOW, GLACIER NATIONAL PARK, MT
As a result of my many trips to Glacier returning to the Logan Pass area when the meadows were in bloom became a priority to me. This particular summer my timing was right on. I love the detail that a large format camera can capture in the Indian Paintbrush flower yet simultaneously keep the mountain in focus. After I took this photo I had a great time talking to the Creator about the beauty that surrounded me. Later that day, at Ptarmigan Tunnel; I lost my wide angle lens, which was the lens I used to take this image!

PAGE 37 HECETA HEAD LIGHTHOUSE, OR
This is a scene that is frequently photographed by both tourists and natives alike. The convenience of this dramatic vista is the reason why. Just step out of your car at the convenient pull-out on Highway 101 and snap a photo. I've actually seen people take this picture without ever leaving their car! But this afternoon was special. The combination of the cirrus cloud drifting overhead and the clear, warm light made for one of my favorite images of the Oregon coast.

PAGE 38 WONDER LAKE, DENALI NATIONAL PARK, AK
Mt. McKinley is our nation's highest peak. But what most people don't know is; McKinley shows the tallest relief of any mountain in the world! That is; the amount of mountain you actually see, from base to summit, is taller than any other mountain. It is a rare thing to have brilliant, clear weather in Denali during the summer months when most people visit the Park. This image was made in early September when the tundra was dressed in gorgeous autumn color. It was 71 degrees and the mosquitoes had returned to whatever pit spawned them. For me, a nature photographer, it doesn't get much better than this. It was an amazing day in a spectacular place.

PAGE 39 GLACIER PEAK WILDERNESS, WA
On my first trip into this pristine area of northern Washington I hitched a ride with an outfitter, who took me on horseback 13 miles to Middle Ridge, where he was supplying a party that had hired his services for the next five days. I set up my tent about a quarter mile from their camp and explored. As I waited for the light to make this image, one of the men hiked over and invited me to join them for dinner. I accepted. When I finished working I was treated to the greatest feast I have ever experienced deep in the wilderness! Jambalaya, (a Cajun dish with fresh shrimp, scallops, and chicken) salad, cheese cake, all freshly made! These are foods I had never associated with backpacking. I was astonished. It was awesome.

PAGE 40 LAKE O'HARA, YOHO NATIONAL PARK, CANADA
Bob and I arrived at the Lake Louise area of the Canadian Rockies around 4:00 am. The following day we went into Lake O'Hara, set up camp and proceeded to hike up the Wiwaxy Trail. The Wiwaxy Trail is a brutally steep climb, (503 meters gained in 1.9 kilometers!) but the sky was clearing and the possibility of a photo was good. About ¾ of the way up we stopped and during the next several hours I took 6 images as the light and clouds constantly changed.

PAGE 41 BAYS LAKE AND MT. JEFFERSON, OR
Probably the question I am asked most frequently is; "Where is your favorite place?" It is a difficult question, to be sure. But in Oregon, Jefferson Park, a square mile of lakes and meadow at the foot of Mt. Jefferson, is at the top of my list. This was where I took my son for his first backpacking trip. I try to go here every year, whether I photograph or not. Most every view of the mountain is a postcard. I think it's hard to *not* take a good picture here!

PAGE 42 YOSEMITE NATIONAL PARK, CA
Yosemite holds a special place in my heart and for many reasons is probably my favorite National Park in the United States. Ansel Adams has enlightened millions to the beauty of Yosemite through his marvelous images. One of his classics is, *Clearing Winter Storm*, which was taken from the Valley view. On this winter morning, I was fortunate enough to experience the same type of conditions he had. And though my work will never be to the standard he set, my inclusion of this image represents not only my love for Yosemite, but my respect for Ansel Adams.

PAGE 43 SMITH ROCKS, OR
I have photographed Smith Rocks State Park on many occasions. During these many visits I made a note that this view of the Crooked River, which flows through and around the park, would be photographed best in spring because of the way morning light hit the rock formations. Consequently, one spring morning I woke up at 3:30 am in order to be at the park for sunrise. The weatherman had previously assured me this morning would bring clearing skies. When I arrived on the eastern side of the Cascades I saw few patches of blue and lots and lots of clouds. By the time I entered the park the sun was playing hide and seek with the clouds. This made for wonderful light and shadow! I was the only one there. It was a delightful morning.

PAGE 44 MAROON BELLS, CO
Early in my career, I visited this area near Aspen, Colorado. My first evening there I camped just down the road from the lake. I remember vividly the violent thunderstorm that rolled through the mountains and my growing disappointment of missing the image I longed to capture. At dawn it was pouring. A few hours later, when the rain finally stopped, I packed quickly, thankful for my reprieve. One last look at the lake before moving on was all I intended. I arrived at the parking lot and the storm was beginning to clear. A fresh coat of snow was draped across the mountains. My disappointment turned into joy! I learned many valuable lessons that day. Not the least of them being the sovereignty of God and patience.

PAGE 46 KEY SUMMIT, NEW ZEALAND
At the beginning (or the end, depending on which direction you begin your trek) of the Roteburn Trek in New Zealand is Key Summit, in Fiordland National Park. The weather here can be nasty, and usually is. But when you have a clear day it has to be one of the most beautiful spots in the world. It's a short steep hike from the road, but the reward more than makes up for the effort. The light that night was awesome.

Page 47   Eiger Peak, Switzerland
When I landed in Frankfurt, Germany I rented a car and immediately drove 5 hours to Interlaken, Switzerland. It was a dismal, grey day. About 40 kilometers from the town the rain turned to snow. I checked into a room and began waiting for the eventual clearing I knew would come. After 3 days of continual snow, my desperately boring vigil ended. I awoke at 4:30 am, took the first train up to Grindelwald where the snow was 3½ feet deep on the cars! The ski lift operator understood enough of my English to allow me an early ride with the employees of the ski lodge. The temperature was 4 degrees F. With every breath, the hairs in my nose would freeze until I exhaled! I spent the day on snowshoes photographing till sundown. On the 30 minute train ride back to Interlaken I fell asleep in the warm embrace of my seat utterly satisfied. I had just enjoyed one of the most beautiful days in my life. It was worth the wait!

Page 48   Berchtesgaden, Germany
On my first visit to Germany I was fortunate enough to run into several days of brilliant fall weather. I spent three of those days hiking around the Königssee, a lake in the middle of the Alps that looks like a fiord. I took this photograph on my way to the top, where I spent a long, cold night in my sleeping bag on a bench.

Page 49   Mt. Rainier National Park, WA
Even though I live in Oregon I have to admit that my favorite mountain in the Cascade Range is Mt. Rainier. This view is from Moraine Park on the north side of the mountain, about a six or seven mile hike. The mosquitoes were particularly bad that summer. I remember sweating like I was in a sauna because I was completely covered to keep those blood thirsty insects at bay. I waited until just before the lake became covered in shadow to make this image.

Page 50   Monument Valley, Yibechi Rocks, AZ
It was the color and texture of the sand that caught my eye in Monument Valley that evening. I had planned to photograph the Yibechi rocks the next morning when there was a more direct light on the rock formations. I was just wandering around that evening hoping to find something striking or unusual. Literally 1 minute after I took this image the sunlight was gone.

Page 53   Punchbowl Falls, OR
In the spring, when the sky is overcast and the wind is calm I make my way to the Columbia River Gorge. The perfect conditions at the perfect time of year to capture the beauty of the dozens of waterfalls swollen with the spring rains and snowmelt from the Cascades. Most of the trails to the waterfalls are short so I tend to go alone on these day hikes. These places offer me the solitude and serenity that allow me quiet moments with my Creator. I often return refreshed as though my soul just took a shower. I am deeply grateful for these times.

Page 54   Sedona, AZ
I was hiking off Schnebly Road, just outside of Sedona when I came across this pool of water in the red rock. Thunderheads were building in the distance, and 5 minutes after I took this picture I got soaked as I returned to my car.

Page 55   Ansel Adams Wilderness, CA
My first and only time (so far!) into this pristine and spectacular part of the Sierras. This is one of those spots where I could easily linger for many days. I love the light on the water. If it weren't for the mosquitoes, this would have been the perfect spot for dinner!

Page 56   Fallen Leaves, ME
On one of my many trips to New England I remember there was constant rain for several days. I was feeling a little desperate to find a picture before I flew home. Though still cloudy, I got a break from the rain and began investigating the landscape. I came upon a lake that had promise of color but there were too many homes dotting the shoreline. As I returned to my car I noticed the ground was covered with pine needles mixed with fallen leaves. I found what I thought was the best color and took this close up.

Page 57   Lake Gunn, Fiordland National Park, New Zealand
One of the marvelous attractions of New Zealand is that many of its natural wonders are easily seen from the road. Though I do a tremendous amount of hiking, New Zealand offers breathtaking scenery for those who are unable to venture into the backcountry. My objective that glorious morning was to photograph Milford Sound, probably the crown jewel among New Zealand's natural gems. I barely noticed passing Lake Gunn on my way as it was shrouded in fog. But when I returned later that morning most of the fog had burned off and I was presented with this image. I call it my unexpected bonus.

Page 58   Redwood National Park, CA
When you walk among the giant redwoods you experience a sense of reverence immediately. They are, after all, the tallest living things on our planet. It is difficult to capture their size with even the widest of lens. Unless you put something in the photo for scale, the tremendous size of the trees is lost. Being a nature photographer, I didn't want to use a man-made object so I used the sunlit sapling in the middle of the photo for scale. It is about 12 feet tall.

PAGE 59 PYRAMID LAKE, NV
Pyramid Lake is a desert lake located about an hour northeast of Reno, NV. I arrived at the lake in dawn's early light to discover a windless morning. The numerous clouds drifted lazily about, waiting for the sun to jump start their day. The color of sunrise never happened and the scene didn't hold much promise for a photograph. I lingered anyway, hoping I might get something for my effort. As the sun ascended in the sky I noticed its light was striking the water from behind the clouds and reflecting back up to illuminate the bottom of a cloud directly in front of me. I searched in vain for a foreground to give my picture a perspective of depth. I noticed this tree limb in the water and sprinted to frame it in the surreal light. It contributes to the image a powerful sense for the viewer that this is a desert lake. My wife loves this picture. She thinks it's "artsy".

PAGE 60 SUNSET, COLUMBIA RIVER, OR
At least once a year since 1995, Bob Dorsey joins me backpacking for a photo trip into the wilderness. He's not a photographer, he just loves the outdoors. He has become a good friend and backpacking partner. In the summer of 2004 we were nearing the end of an 8 day backpack in Wyoming. After driving about 12 hours we were within an hour of home when I noticed a high overcast with a small clearing on the Western horizon. I told Bob that the sky looked like it might be a great sunset, but he was anxious to see his wife. I was too, but this scene looked ripe with possibilities. After depositing Bob with his wife I returned to the Columbia river. As I drove I phoned Terri and reluctantly told her I'd be a little late. The sky developed into one of those rare sunsets when God lights the heavens from west to east as though they are on fire. And though it delayed my homecoming, I'm thankful I went back. By the way, my wife understood. She is great!

PAGE 61 GLEN ETIVE, SCOTLAND
Usually when I visit a new area I spend a lot of time in a car exploring with no particular destination in mind. Just looking and getting a feel for the landscape. I had gone to Scotland in June because of the long days (20 hours of daylight) and the lush green of Spring in the Northern Highlands. What attracted me to this image was the Rhododendron in bloom. I was unaware that to get in a position where I could photograph the flowers with the lake and the mountains as my focal point I would have to slog through mud over a foot deep. I was a mess. This made for an extended clean up in a nearby creek, but I think the picture was worth it.

PAGE 62 CHESTER COUNTY, PA
I grew up in southeastern Pennsylvania and spent much of my life in this area. This photo sparks many memories for me. My good friend Randy was with me as we drove through the countryside in search of photo opportunities. I love this particular image because I feel I actually captured a typical autumn day in Chester County (at least according to my memories). It really does look like this. Rolling hills, manicured pastureland, hazy but clear sunshine, distant color in the leaves—it was the perfect day for a Sunday afternoon drive.

PAGE 63 WAIKOLOA, HI
This image almost didn't make the final cut for the book. After dozens of reviews and edits I realized that I had no photos of Hawaii, which is one of my favorite places on earth. I chose this image because of the incredible nuances of color in the sky and because it looks so "Hawaiian". Relaxing next to a beach, enjoying tropical breezes, sipping a pineapple drink, and watching a gorgeous sunset so that I might capture the moment on film is a demanding job. Now if all the photographs would be this tough

PAGE 64 LAKE WANAKA, NEW ZEALAND
New Zealand is so spectacular! It was difficult to choose which images would represent the diverse beauty of that country. This is the far western end of Lake Wanaka which you pass on your way to Mt. Aspiring Park. On my last morning of a 10 day visit I was retuning to Queenstown to catch my departing flight. The rugged peaks, the lush greens, the pastureland, the unique blue of New Zealand water, and the vibrant flowers together represent New Zealand well. But it was the marvelous light that convinced me to take this photograph. Every time I look at this image I remember how difficult it was to leave.

PAGE 65 DOUBLE ARCH, ARCHES NATIONAL PARK, UT
Though I have what I believe is one of the greatest jobs on the planet, it is not always what people imagine it to be. The bulk of my job takes a generous portion of patience and persistence. This is a photo that I attempted to film on 3 separate days before this image was actually made. The last rays of evening light turn the red sandstone even redder. Because this arch faces the western sky I knew it would be a prime location for me at the end of the day. But on my 3 previous attempts clouds hung about the western horizon blocking the best light of the day. Finally, a clear evening showed how red the rock could become! I'm glad I went a fourth time.

PAGE 66 SHENANDOAH NATIONAL PARK, VA
Shenandoah National Park is a great place to visit, especially in autumn. The goal for this photograph was to capture the autumn color sweeping down the mountain to the valley below. The afternoon light was the time to make the image. I love the detail of the rock in the foreground. After I made the image I enjoyed dinner here!

PAGE 67 ONEONTA GORGE, OR
This is one of my favorite spots in the Columbia River Gorge. It's an easy walk up the stream (but the water is cold). If you happen to be there on a spring day when the sun is high, it pierces the gorge and lights up the wall. I shot the wall instead of the opening because it provides a perspective that gives a more realistic sense of its size and beauty.

Page 68 Mt. Triglav, Slovenia
I have some good friends who are missionaries in the small, beautiful country of Slovenia. I have had the privilege of visiting them on several occasions and assisting them in the work there. On a sparkling clear winter day Josh took me searching for photo possibilities. I'm not quite sure where we ended up, but we found a view of Triglav (Slovenia's highest peak) in the distance across a snow covered farmers field. We waited for the sun to color the clouds and took this shot. Good people, good friends, good memories, beautiful planet.

Page 69 Todd Lake and Mt. Bachelor, OR
When my good friend, Don Miller, first moved into our home he expressed interest in going on a photo trip someday. So, one morning, about 1:30am, he joined me for a short day trip to central Oregon (I don't think Don ever went to sleep that night). From our home, Todd Lake is a 3½ hour drive. We arrived with plenty of time to find the right spot to compose the photo. I waited for the sun to brush the trees with its golden color. I made two exposures and knew I had the image I wanted. Though Don said he enjoyed the hike, he never returned on any early morning trips. He says he prefers evening light.

Page 70 Upper Multnomah Falls, OR
This was my first photo of a waterfall that I knew was a "keeper". I remember being so excited that I had done a respectable job in capturing the beauty that I had encountered there. I am often asked, "What makes a good nature photograph?" Of course, many technical, compositional, and "uniqueness" issues could be discussed. But one criterion is undeniable: Does the image create within the viewer a desire to go there? For me, almost two decades have passed since I took this photo. And I still want to go there.

Page 71 Three Sisters Wilderness, OR
I remember ascending a trail for 3 miles that leveled and spilled out into a large meadow. The profusion of wildflowers was amazing! I dropped my pack and searched in vain for a vantage point to best capture this multi-hued living carpet. I settled on a close up of a particular cluster of intensely colored Indian Paintbrush. Most times, I'm looking for the "big" picture. But there is beauty in the small as well.

Page 72 Cape Meares, OR
What I enjoy most about this image is the amazing color. To appreciate how unique this is, consider my experience. In the hundreds of visits I have made to the Oregon coast I have witnessed color like this maybe a half dozen times!

Page 73 Wallowa Lake, OR
Wallowa Lake is at the foot of the Eagle Cap Wilderness in the northeast corner of Oregon. Because of it's "out of the way" location it remains unseen and unknown and to most visitors. But natives of our wonderful State know the beauty of these mountains. Shortly after I photographed the suns' first light that morning, clouds began to drift past the peaks and the lake became still. I waited a little bit for the clouds to get into a better position and took this shot.

Page 74 Noosa National Park, Australia
On my first trip to Australia, Terri joined me. When we were younger, and without kids, this was often the case. We were fortunate to visit and hike around Noosa National Park to see the Koala bears that inhabit the forest there. Though we did see the bears, none of them cooperated with my efforts to take their picture. As the sunset rapidly approached, I discovered this flower. The color was muted because of haze on the horizon but cast a beautiful light on this scene. I have great memories of this trip. Specifically, my wife at my side.

Page 75 Hurricane Ridge, Olympic National Park, WA
A paved road makes Hurricane Ridge easily accessible to the tens of thousands of visitors every summer at Olympic National Park. Even so, in the numerous times over the years that I have visited there I have only encountered a hand full of people in this particular meadow. The view from this vantage point is one of the best in the Northwest. Rows of forested ridges stretch into the distance with snow capped peaks as a backdrop and meadows carpeted with flowers as a foreground. This image was taken only a few minutes before the sun dropped below the horizon. I love the golden light on the hillside. It is my favorite time of day.

Page 76 Long Pond, ME
The first time I went to Maine was in the autumn of 1998. It had been raining most of my time there. As I was driving I was searching my map. I finally located some lakes I thought might provide a good scenic image. But the waning light and unfamiliar territory added a sense of urgency to my task. I finally parked my car and raced the daylight to the lake. Thick forest crowded the shoreline. Sweating and out of breath, I found beautiful maple trees but their color was muted due to the overcast. I was about to turn back when suddenly the sun broke from behind the clouds. It was a magical light. The kind of light that only happens immediately following a rain. It seemed to color the air itself and the forest exploded with color! I took two photos and the sun disappeared for the rest of the evening.

PAGE 77   CLACKAMAS RIVER, OR
I was on my way to Central Oregon with my friend Rick to play golf for the weekend when I began to notice flowers blooming along the road. I rounded a bend and saw this profusion of lupine on a hillside descending to the Clackamas River. Fortunately, I have learned to take my camera almost everywhere I go. This shot to me is quintessential Oregon. The light, the trees, the flowers, the river, the lushness of the landscape is why I live here.

PAGE 78   BEACH ROCKS, OLYMPIC NATIONAL PARK, WA
When the fog (so typical of Northwest beaches) began to roll in, I started back to my car. As I was walking across the slick rocks along the beach I began noticing some really neat colors and patterns. I found some that particularly drew my interest and took a couple of photos. Beauty was underneath my feet! It pays to always be looking.

PAGE 79   ACADIA NATIONAL PARK, ME
This is my favorite location for the sunrise on the eastern coast of our country. I think it's because it reminds me of the Oregon coast. After sunrise I'm usually off to find autumn color somewhere in the Park. I was fortunate to still be here on this particular morning to capture the beautiful cirrus clouds lined in perfect symmetry with the coastline.

PAGE 80   GRINDELWALD, SWITZERLAND
Whenever my friends see this image they break out in "The hills are alive with Sound of Music…" I think that's all they know of the tune. Problem is; this image is in Switzerland not Austria. What you see is the north face of the Eiger, one of the classic climbs in the Alps. Maybe my friends should break out with a tune from *The Eiger Sanction*, but I doubt they've ever seen it.

PAGE 81   TORONGO RIVER, AUSTRALIA
I was visiting a good friend of mine, Bill Vassiliou, who took me on a hike to Torongo Falls. On our way back along the river, the enormous size of the giant ferns and the lushness of the forest caught my eye. After I took this photo I fell in the river. Bill reminds me every time I talk with him of how much of a clod I am.

PAGE 82   COLUMBIA RIVER GORGE, OR
I was playing tourist guide for my sister, Judy, who was visiting from the East Coast and took her to the Columbia River Gorge. A must stop for any good guide. It had been raining so photographs were not part of the plan. We rounded a corner and saw flowers in bloom, so I reluctantly stopped to let Judy soak in the scene. She was gushing about how beautiful everything was and to me it was just another average day in Oregon. (What do foreigners know anyway?) But when we got out of the car I immediately noticed the stillness, which is highly unusual for the Gorge. Ignoring the loud groans of protest, I pulled out my camera and made this image. I love the droplets of water on the leaves from the earlier rain. I guess foreigners know something after all.

PAGE 83   LAKE TAHOE, NV
This image was actually made in the middle of February! I had planned a trip to Tahoe for winter photos and when I arrived, there was no snow. It looks more like April or May. What makes it unique is not just the "way cool" clouds drifting overhead, but the angle of the sunlight. If the picture was taken in the spring you would never get this light. The angle is different. This is a winter sun. And it makes all the difference!

BACK JACKET COVER   GLEN COE, SCOTLAND
I spent several days in this area of the Highlands and this image was made on the singular day of clear skies. Memories of this place are strong for me. I had been away from my family for almost two weeks and was missing them terribly. While I was scrambling up this hill I heard a strange sound. From some where down the valley a Scotsman (in full dress I later found out) was playing the bagpipes. As his notes drifted toward me I recognized the tune. It was *Amazing Grace*. It was an experience unlike any I've had before or since. As my eyes absorbed the wonderful scene before me, my ears were serenaded with music that reminded me of powerful lyric and stirred my soul. Becoming emotional as I listened alone for some 20–30 minutes, I still remember asking myself "Is this what heaven might be like?" As my friend for life, John Woodall is fond of saying; it is an etched memory.

Be sure to look for John MacMurray's first collection of stunning photographs in his book entitled,

By Chance?
Landscapes from the canvas of the Creator

Check your local bookstore or go to:

www.creationcalendars.com